THINK and SOLVE

1

HAROLD CLARKE
ROBERT SHEPHERD

CAMBRIDGE
UNIVERSITY PRESS

Designed and illustrated by Celia Hart
Cover design by Chris McLeod

Published by the Press Syndicate of the University of Cambridge
The Pitt Building, Trumpington Street, Cambridge CB2 1RP
40 West 20th Street, New York, NY 10011–4211, USA
10 Stamford Road, Oakleigh, Melbourne 3166, Australia

First published 1984
Tenth printing 1994

Printed in Great Britain at the University Press, Cambridge

ISBN 0 521 26971 7

RD

Task 1

1 Add together 5 and 7.

2 Take 3 from 10.

3 7 × 2.

4 Add 12 and 6.

5 Share 12 by 3.

6 Put these in order, smallest first: 17,   21,   19.

7 6 + ☐ = 10.

8 Multiply 3 by 10.

9 Write **thirty-seven** in figures.

10 What is one more than 19?

11 How many corners are there in a square?

12 Is 8 an even number?

13 How many minutes are there in a ¼ of an hour?

14 How many days are there in a week?

15 What is twice four?

16 David had 11 toffees. He ate 4.
How many did he have left?

17 One bag has 8 sweets and another has 5 sweets.
How many sweets are there altogether?

18 There are three vases, each with 7 roses.
How many roses are there altogether? 21

19 14 boys and 9 girls live in our street.
How many children is that altogether?

20 There are 20 nails in a packet.
How many nails are there in 3 packets?

Task 2

1 Add together 6 and 9.

2 What is 20 take away 4?

3 What are 3 lots of five?

4 What is 8p less than 20p?

5 Find half of 10.

6 How many tens are there in forty?

7 Take 10 from 45.

8 What is one less than 30?

9 $4 + \square = 10$.

10 Write **twenty-four** in figures.

11 What is the next number?   2,   4,   6,   ?

12 What shape is this page?

13 Which day comes two days after Wednesday?

14 Is 5 an even number?

15 How many months are there in a year?

16 Susan is 12 years old.
How old was she 5 years ago?

17 A bus can carry 25 people.
How many people can two buses carry?

18 Two cakes are cut into quarters.

into
quarters

How many quarters are there?

19 Daniel has 50p. He buys a jigsaw for 45p.
What change does he get?

20 What is the cost of four ice-creams at 15p each?

Task 3

A

1 Find the sum of 7 and 8.

2 What is 16 take away 7?

3 What is $3 + 4 + 5$?

4 Multiply 4 by 4.

5 Share 18 by 3.

6 Put these in order, smallest first: 16,   8,   11.

7 $\square + 2 = 10$.

8 How many tens are there in 50?

9 What is ten more than 26?

10 $5 \times \boxed{10} = 50$.

B

11 Is this 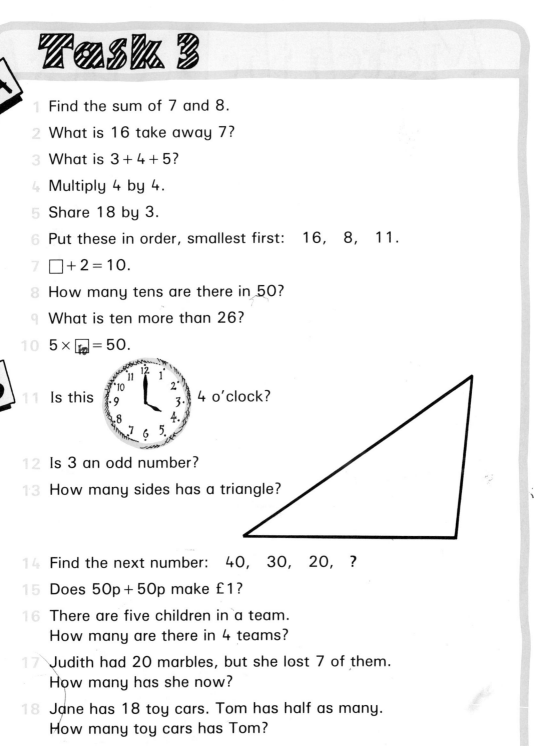 4 o'clock?

12 Is 3 an odd number?

13 How many sides has a triangle?

14 Find the next number: 40,   30,   20,   ?

15 Does $50p + 50p$ make £1?

16 There are five children in a team.
     How many are there in 4 teams?

17 Judith had 20 marbles, but she lost 7 of them.
     How many has she now?

18 Jane has 18 toy cars. Tom has half as many.
     How many toy cars has Tom?

19 Three apples are cut into halves.
     How many halves are there altogether?

20 How many 10p stamps can I buy with 50p?

Match the beetles!

Each beetle has to find a partner to make a pair. Their partner has the same number of dots on its back.

If you think A goes with E, write A, E.

Task 4

1 Add together 5 and 8.

2 15 − 8.

3 What are 3 lots of 4?

4 Add 5p to 12p.

5 What is half of 16?

6 What is one more than 29?

7 What is ten more than 34?

8 Write **32** in words.

9 10 − ☐ = 6.

10 How many tens are there in 70?

11 Which day is 3 days after Saturday?

12 What is the next number?   5,   10,   15,   ?

13 Does 5p + 10p + 5p make 20p?

14 How many days are there in a fortnight?

15 What shape is a hoop?

16 Mary gave me 5 sweets. Sally gave me 7 sweets.
How many was I given altogether?

17 John is 11 years old. How old was he 4 years ago?

18 Three bags each have 9 plums in them.
How many plums are there altogether?

19 Robert had 14 marbles, but he lost 5 of them.
How many has he now?

20 Jill had a 50p piece. She spent 30p.
How much had she left?

Task 5

A

1 Find the sum of 3 and 9.

2 16 − 9.

3 3 × 6.

4 Share 12 into 3 lots. How many are there in each lot?

5 What is 4 + 3 + 2?

6 Add ten to 31.

7 5 + ☐ = 10.

8 Write **twenty-six** in figures.

9 Multiply 4 by 10.

10 Put these in order, smallest first: 41,   18,   21.

B

11 Is this 7 o'clock?   *yes*

12 Is 12 an even number?

13 Are we asleep at 3 a.m.?

'a.m.' means 'in the morning'. 'p.m.' means 'in the afternoon'.

14 What is double eight?

15 Which three coins make 8p?

16 Phil shared 30 marbles between himself and two of his friends. How many did they each have?

17 Dawn had 15 cherries. She ate 7. How many had she left?

18 If I get 30p pocket money and I buy a comic for 25p, how much have I left?

19 Sandy has 5 cars, each having 4 wheels. How many wheels are there altogether?

20 Mum gave Tommy 14p, and Dad gave him 12p. How much was he given altogether?

Task 6

A

1 Add 6 to 7.

2 Take 4 from 11.

3 What is $4 + 5 + 6$?

4 Find 5×2.

5 Share 18 by 2.

6 How many tens are there in 30?

7 $10 - \square = 3$.

8 What is one more than 32?

9 Write **38** in words.

10 Take ten from 39.

B

11 Is this [rectangle] a rectangle? *yes*

12 Find the missing compass point.
North, East, South, ?

13 What is the next number? 3, 5, 7, 9, ?

14 Is this [clock] half past three?

15 Which day is two days before Tuesday?

16 Six children each ate 3 sandwiches.
How many sandwiches did they eat altogether?

17 Five children were away, but 24 were there.
How many are in that class?

18 It takes 7 minutes to walk to the bus stop, and
the bus ride takes 12 minutes.
How long is the journey altogether?

19 Six grapefruit are cut into halves.
How many halves are there altogether?

20 What is the cost of 4 apples at 7p each?

7

Task 7

1 Add together 4 and 8.

2 $15 - 7$.

3 Find 4 lots of 4.

4 Add 9p to 8p.

5 What is half of 14?

6 Write **28** in words.

7 Put these in order, smallest first: 23, 17, 26.

8 Take 10 from 34.

9 $1 + \square = 10$.

10 Take one from 26.

11 How many corners has a triangle?

12 Does this clock read a quarter to 12?

13 Is 16 an odd number?

14 Which three coins make 5p?

15 What is the next number? 7, 5, 3, ?

16 Soldiers stand 8 in a row.
How many are there in 3 rows?

17 Jason is 14 years old. How old was he 5 years ago?

18 Jenny had twelve mints. After giving some away
she had 4 left. How many did she give away?

19 Peter had 20p. He bought a sweet for 11p.
How much had he left?

20 20 bottles fill a crate.
How many bottles are there in 4 full crates?

Ladder adders

Add up the numbers on each number ladder.

Task 8

1 Add together 5 and 9.

2 What is 14 take away 8?

3 Find half of 12.

4 3×6.

5 Add 6p to 12p.

6 Write **46** in words.

7 Add one to 44.

8 Which is the largest number in this list? 19, 47, 24, 11.

9 $10 - \square = 4$.

10 Take 10 from 27.

11 Is 42 an even number?

12 Is this [ ] a square?

13 Which month follows June?

14 Do some people have breakfast at 8a.m.?

15 Which day is 3 days before Friday?

16 Six tennis balls fit in a box.
How many balls are there in 4 boxes?

17 Wasim had 15p pocket money, and then he found 5p.
How much has he now?

18 Anne has 4 dolls, and Rosie has twice as many.
How many does Rosie have?

19 In a class there are thirteen boys and fifteen girls.
How many children are there altogether?

20 In the same class, 4 children were away.
How many of the class were at school?

 **Task 9**

1 What is the sum of 6 and 6?

2 18 − 7.

3 Multiply 3 by 2.

4 Share 21 by 3.

5 Add together 9p and 4p.

6 $2 + \square + 5 = 10$.

7 Put these in order, largest first: 41, 7, 25.

8 Take one from 41.

9 $3 \times \square = 30$.

10 Add ten to 36.

11 Which month follows September?

12 How many sides has a rectangle?

13 Which three coins make 7p?

14 Is 17 an odd number?

15 Are you at school at 9:30 p.m.?

16 Tim had 16 felt-tipped pens, but seven of them ran dry. How many were left?

17 How many five-a-side teams can be made from 20 boys?

18 3 apples are cut into quarters. How many quarters are there?

19 Rubbers cost 6p each. How much will 5 rubbers cost?

20 There are 40 pages in a book, and Sarah has read 15 of them. How many pages has she still to read?

Task 10

1 Find the sum of 7 and 3.

2 Take 4 from 13.

3 Share 15 by 3.

4 Add $2 + 4 + 6$.

5 Multiply 5 by 4.

6 Write **thirty-six** in figures.

7 Add one to 39.

8 Take 10 from 43.

9 $\square + 3 + 4 = 10$.

10 Which is the smallest number? 34, 14, 27, 17.

11 Does this clock read a quarter past four?

12 Which month follows February?

13 How many sides has a square?

14 Fill in the missing compass point.
North, ?, South, West.

15 What is twice nine?

16 A chocolate bar has six pieces to it.
How many pieces are there in three bars?

17 Theresa has 30 marbles, and Devina has half as many.
How many has Devina?

18 Three boxes each hold 20 pencils.
How many pencils are there altogether?

19 I get 50p pocket money. If I spend 35p,
how much have I left?

20 Bill had 17 conkers, but Ian gave him 8 more.
How many has Bill now?

Similar Shapes

Say which shapes are similar to A, B, C, D and E.
Match the letters with the numbers.

Task 11

A

1 Add together 4 and 9.

2 Take 8 from 11.

3 Add 7p to 12p.

4 7×3.

5 Find two lots of 6.

6 $10 - \square = 2$.

7 Take one from 20.

8 Write **39** in words.

9 Put these in order, largest first: 17,   21,   13.

10 Take 10 from 47.

B

11 Are shops open at 11 a.m. on Saturday morning?

12 Which is the last month of the year?

13 How many corners has a rectangle?

14 Which three coins make 13p?

15 What is the next number?   3,   6,   9,   ?

16 Farmer Giles had 18 cows in a field.
11 got out one day. How many stayed behind?

17 There are 15 blue ribbons and 8 green ones.
How many ribbons are there altogether?

18 One pencil costs 7p. How much will 3 pencils cost?

19 Paul shared his stamps with his two brothers.
If there were 24 stamps, how many did they each get?

20 Doris has 20 sweets, and Hansa has half as many.
How many has Hansa?

Task 12

A

1 Add together 5 and 10.

2 From 12 take 9.

3 What are 5 lots of 4?

4 3×4.

5 What is half of 14?

6 Write **37** in words.

7 $10 = 4 + 2 + \square$.

8 $5 \times 10 = \square$.

9 Take one from 40.

10 Add ten to 32.

B

11 Is 36 an even number?

12 Does this clock read 7:30?

13 Which month follows March?

14 Which day is 4 days before Monday?

15 Which three coins make 9p?

16 There are 5 children in a team.
How many are there in six teams?

17 Mark had 15 minutes' playtime.
He played football for 8 minutes.
How long was left?

18 Pauline is 11 years old.
How old will she be in 7 years' time?

19 Luke has 40p. If he spends 25p,
How much will he have left?

20 Six balls fill a box.
How many boxes can be filled with 60 balls?

Task 13

A

1 Add together 7 and 9.

2 Take 5 from 19.

3 3×8.

4 Find half of 18.

5 If one toffee costs 9p, how much do 3 toffees cost?

6 $10 - \square = 8$.

7 Take ten from 62.

8 Which two of these numbers add up to
   ten?   7,   4,   3.

9 What is one more than 79?

10 10×12.

B

11 Which is larger, 3×6 or 4×4?

12 If today is Saturday,
   in how many days will it be Wednesday?

13 Is 43 an even number?

14 Is this shape cut into halves? ———————————

15 Which month follows July?

16 Julie and Sue were picking flowers.
   Julie picked 13, while Sue picked 8.
   How many flowers were picked altogether?

17 What is the cost of three oranges at 7p each?

18 20 pegs are in a packet.
   How many pegs are there in 4 packets?

19 Seven grapefruit are cut into halves.
   How many halves are there?

20 Richard had 15p, but a 5p coin and a 2p coin rolled
   away. How much had he left?

Task 14

A

1 Add together 8 and 11.

2 Take six from 17.

3 Share 9 by 3.

4 Find two lots of 4.

5 Spencer has 4 marbles, but Derek has 7.
How many have they altogether?

6 $10 = 1 + 5 + \square$.

7 How many tens are there in 80?

8 Put these in order, smallest first: 37, 42, 29.

9 Write **53** in words.

10 $7 \times \square = 70$.

B

11 Which three coins make 6p?

12 Is this 4:30?

13 Is this shape a circle?

14 What is the next number? 12, 10, 8, 6, ?

15 Is this a clockwise direction?

16 Share 18 pence so that Margaret and Jane get half
each. How much do they get?

17 Helen had 15 acorns in her collection.
If she found nine more, how many would she have?

18 Elizabeth spent some of her 30p pocket money on a
book. She got 15p change. How much was the book?

19 10 bottles fill a crate.
How many crates will 40 bottles fill?

20 Chocolate bars cost 15p each. How much will 4 bars cost?

Starters

In each row start with the one on the left.
Put the next three items in the right order.
Use the letters A, B and C for each answer.

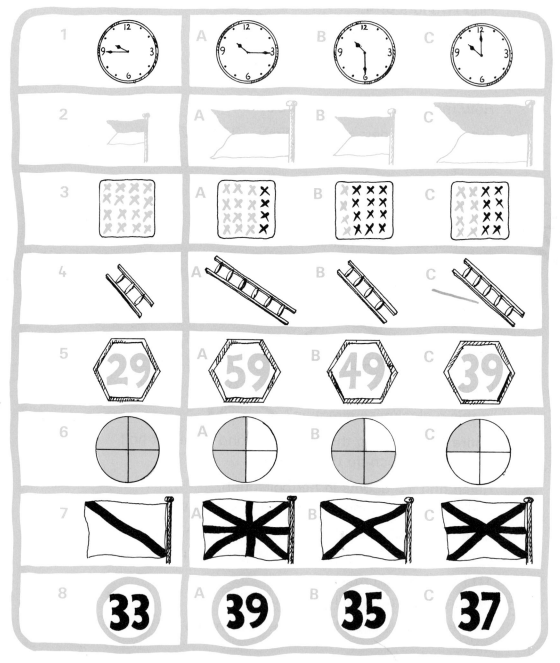

Task 15

A

1 Find the sum of 3 and 12.

2 Take 8 from 12.

3 Add 9p to 12p.

4 Multiply 3 by 5.

5 Share 20 into 5 groups.

6 Take 10 from the largest number
here: 42, 34, 44.

7 Add 1 to 89.

8 What is the value of the 6 in the number 63?

9 10×14.

10 $6 + 1 + \square = 10$.

B

11 How many sides has a triangle?

12 Is half of this
shape coloured?

13 Is the evening news on at 6 a.m.?

14 If today is Tuesday, in how many days will it be Sunday?

15 Which is smaller, $7 + 7$ or $6 + 9$?

16 Karl has 12 toy cars. Ivan has half as many as Karl.
How many toy cars has Ivan?

17 Lee has 18 more pages to fill in his maths book.
When he has finished another 12, how many more
will he have to fill?

18 Balloons cost 4p each. How much will 7 cost?

19 I started work at 6 o'clock and stopped 15 minutes
later. When did I stop?

20 Catherine has reached page 17.
If she reads 12 more pages, which page will she reach?

Task 16

1 Add 5 to 9.

2 13 − 4.

3 Share twelve marbles between two boys.
How many do they each get?

4 What is two times five?

5 Add together 3, 6 and 9.

6 Write **89** in words.

7 How many tens are there in 110?

8 10 − ☐ = 1.

9 Which two of these numbers add up to ten?   2,   5,   8.

10 Add ten to the smallest number here: 35,   53,   33.

11 Which compass direction is missing?
North, East, **?**, West.

12 Is this shape
cut into halves?

13 Is 56 an odd number?

14 How many hours is it from 6 o'clock to 10 o'clock?

15 Which month is just before April?

16 Half the children had sandwiches.
The rest, 7 of them, had rolls.
How many children were there altogether?

17 Alex had 36 stamps. He gave 13 of them to Nicola.
How many had he left?

18 Tony was keeping quiet. He did not say anything for
12 minutes, but after another 12 minutes he said 'Golly'.
For how long was he quiet?

19 70 soldiers were standing 10 to a row.
How many rows were there?

20 Stickers cost 8p each. How much will three stickers cost?

Task 17

A

1 Find the sum of 4 and 13.

2 What is 6 less than 13?

3 I have 16p. If I spend 7p, how much will I have left?

4 Find 4 lots of five.

5 What is half of 18?

6 What is one less than 90?

7 $\square + 5 + 1 = 10$.

8 Multiply 17 by 10.

9 $180 + 10 = \square$.

10 Write **eighty-five** in figures.

B

11 Which month is before March?

12 Is this a cylinder?

13 Which is smaller, 4×4 or 3×5?

14 What is the next number? 20, 16, 12, 8, ?

15 Is this an anticlockwise direction?

16 Gary is 12 years old.
How old will he be in seven years' time?

17 8 grapefruit halves are laid out for breakfast.
How many grapefruit were used?

18 Mrs Finn needed four teams of five children.
How many children did she need?

19 Three children share 18 sweets among themselves.
How many do they each get?

20 Steve had 23p, but a 2p coin and a 10p coin fell
down the drain. How much did he have left?

FLAG TAGS

Find a flag with a letter above.
Match that flag with one just like it below.
Multiply the number in the first flag by
the number in the other one.
Write your answers like this:
A__, B__, C__, and so on.

22

Task 18

A

1 Add 11 to 5.

2 From 15 take 8.

3 What is 2×8?

4 Oranges cost 9p each. How much would 2 oranges cost?

5 Share 16 into 4 groups.

6 How many tens are there in 140?

7 Put these in order, largest first: 38,   43,   37.

8 Take one from 70.

9 What is the value of 9 in 49?

10 What is 10×16?

B

11 Is this 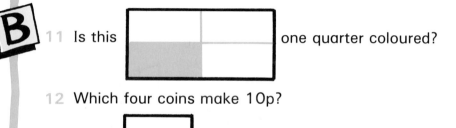 one quarter coloured?

12 Which four coins make 10p?

13 Is this ⬜ a square?

14 How long is it from 7 o'clock until 11 o'clock?

15 Is 47 an odd number?

16 Six children each collected 5p for some flowers for their teacher. How much did they collect altogether?

17 Playtime starts at 2 o'clock. It ends at a quarter past two. How long does it last?

18 Andrew had 20 eggs left for cooking, but 7 fell on the floor. How many were left?

19 How many 10p apples could I buy with 60p?

20 Peggy had 7 felt-tipped pens. Her Dad gave her a new packet of 12. How many had she then?

Task 19

A

1 What is the total of $6 + 12$?

2 $19 - 2$.

3 Find 3×9.

4 If I have 15p and I buy a biscuit for 6p, how much have I left?

5 Share 5 into 20.

6 Add 10 to 84.

7 Which two of these numbers add up to 10?   3,   4,   6,   2.

8 Multiply 13 by 10.

9 Share 160 by 10.

10 Write **48** in words.

B

11 Which is larger, $16 - 6$ or 3×3?

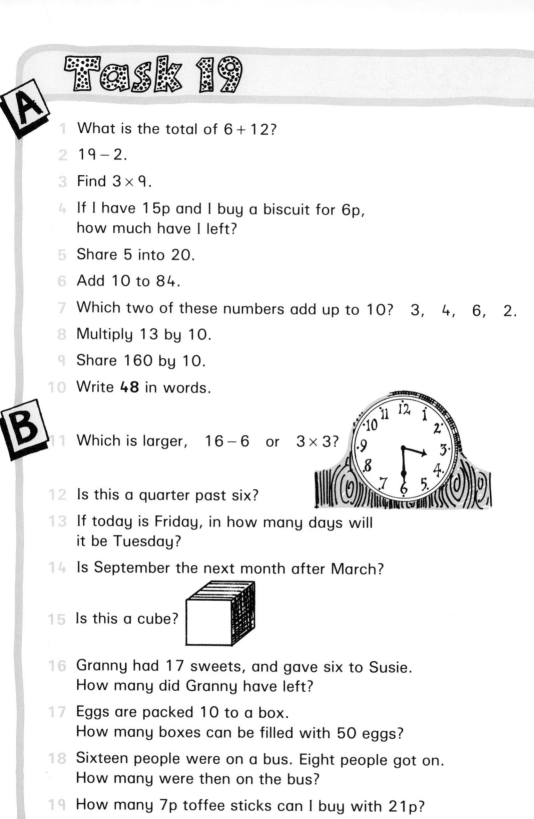

12 Is this a quarter past six?

13 If today is Friday, in how many days will it be Tuesday?

14 Is September the next month after March?

15 Is this a cube?

16 Granny had 17 sweets, and gave six to Susie. How many did Granny have left?

17 Eggs are packed 10 to a box. How many boxes can be filled with 50 eggs?

18 Sixteen people were on a bus. Eight people got on. How many were then on the bus?

19 How many 7p toffee sticks can I buy with 21p?

20 How many 2p pieces make 16p?

Task 20

1. What is 5 + 14?
2. Take 7 from 14.
3. Share 18 by 6.
4. Multiply 7 by 4.
5. Add 3 + 5 + 7.
6. 3 + ☐ + 7 = 10.
7. What is the value of the 9 in 94?
8. What are 10 lots of 22?
9. Write **92** in words.
10. Add ten to 67.

11. Is this a clockwise direction?
12. Does Manchester United play football on Saturdays at 3 a.m.?
13. Is 56 an even number?
14. Is this shape cut into halves?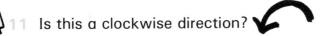
15. What is the next number?   10,   7,   4,   **?**
16. I had 15 minutes to get home, but it only took 11 minutes. How many minutes was I early?
17. Half the class forgot, but the rest remembered. If 15 forgot, how many were in the class?
18. Mr Turner had 4 sets of brushes. Each set had six brushes in it. How many brushes did he have altogether?
19. Angela scored 7 goals last week and 12 this week. How many goals did she score altogether?
20. The 10:15 bus was a quarter of an hour late. When did it arrive?

25

Task 21

1　Find the total of 9 and 8.

2　16 − 5.

3　4 × 6.

4　Share 20 into 2 groups.

5　What are five lots of 5?

6　What is ten more than 81?

7　Share 150 by 10.

8　$5 = 10 - \square$.

9　Take one from 60.

10　Put these in order, smallest first:　72,　43,　38.

11　How long is it from 12 noon until 2 p.m.?

12　Does September follow August?

13　Is this 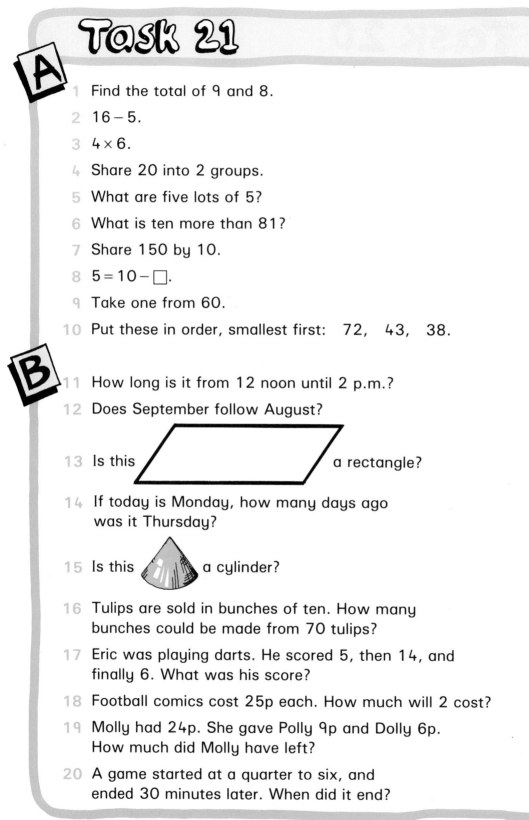 a rectangle?

14　If today is Monday, how many days ago
　　was it Thursday?

15　Is this　a cylinder?

16　Tulips are sold in bunches of ten. How many
　　bunches could be made from 70 tulips?

17　Eric was playing darts. He scored 5, then 14, and
　　finally 6. What was his score?

18　Football comics cost 25p each. How much will 2 cost?

19　Molly had 24p. She gave Polly 9p and Dolly 6p.
　　How much did Molly have left?

20　A game started at a quarter to six, and
　　ended 30 minutes later. When did it end?

Number of children

	Fruit chews	Lollies	Choc Drops	Toffees	Jelly sweets

9
8
7
6
5
4
3
2
1

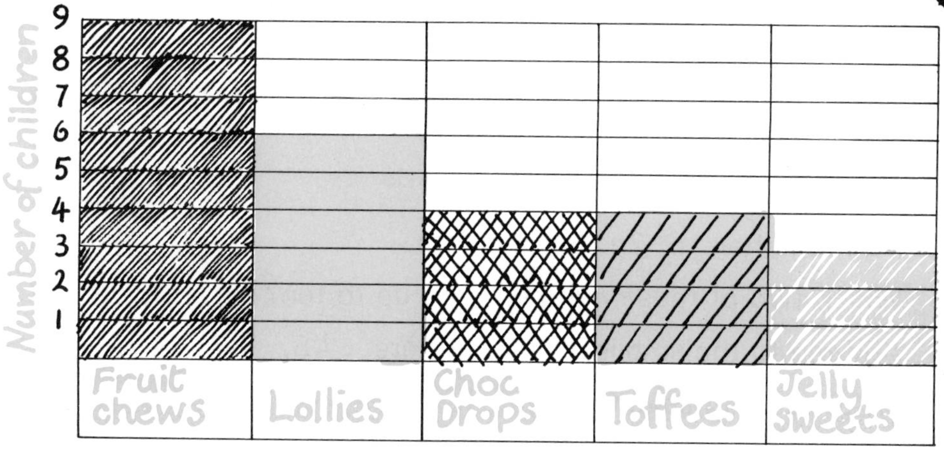

This box picture shows the sweets which

children like best in a class.

Each box means one child.

1 How many children like fruit chews?

2 How many children like jelly sweets?

3 Which two kinds of sweets are liked by
the same number of children?

4 How many children like lollies better than
jelly sweets?

5 How many children like fruit chews better
than choc drops?

6 Which two kinds of sweets added together give
the same number as for fruit chews?

7 How many children altogether like lollies or
fruit chews?

8 How many children are there in the class?

9 There are eleven boys in the class.
How many girls are there?

10 Do half the children in the class like fruit chews or
toffees better than any other sweets?

27

Task 22

A

1 What is the sum of 7 and 13?

2 19 − 11.

3 What are 3 lots of 7?

4 Put 20 conkers into 4 equal piles.
How many are there in each pile?

5 Add together 1p, 2p, 5p and 10p.

6 Which two of these numbers add up to ten?   4,   3,   2,   7.

7 Add ten to the smallest number here: 48,   37,   45.

8 Write **seventy-seven** in figures.

9 How many tens are there in 170?

10 16 × 10.

B

11 Is this 5:15?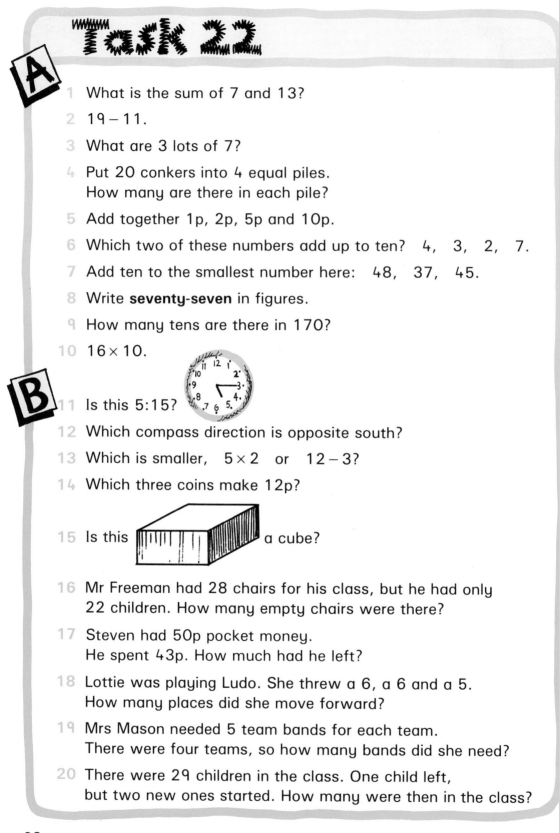

12 Which compass direction is opposite south?

13 Which is smaller,   5 × 2   or   12 − 3?

14 Which three coins make 12p?

15 Is this [cube drawing] a cube?

16 Mr Freeman had 28 chairs for his class, but he had only
22 children. How many empty chairs were there?

17 Steven had 50p pocket money.
He spent 43p. How much had he left?

18 Lottie was playing Ludo. She threw a 6, a 6 and a 5.
How many places did she move forward?

19 Mrs Mason needed 5 team bands for each team.
There were four teams, so how many bands did she need?

20 There were 29 children in the class. One child left,
but two new ones started. How many were then in the class?

Task 23

1 What is the total of 4 and 15?

2 From 17 take 13.

3 Multiply 9 by 3.

4 Sherbets cost 8p each. How much will 2 cost?

5 What change from 20p will I get after buying 2 sherbets?

6 $\square + 3 + 6 = 10$.

7 What are 10 lots of 21?

8 Add one to the largest number here: 41, 49, 45.

9 Take ten from 96.

10 What is the value of the three in 23?

11 Is this a clockwise direction?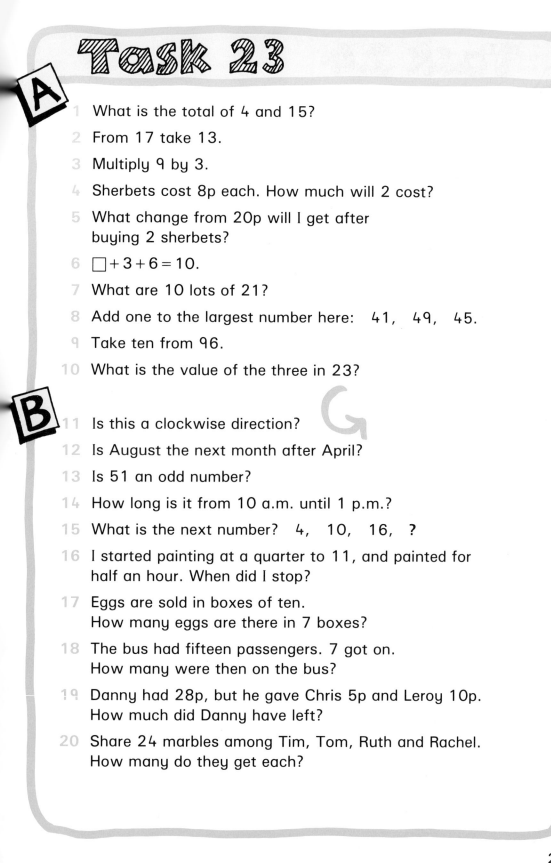

12 Is August the next month after April?

13 Is 51 an odd number?

14 How long is it from 10 a.m. until 1 p.m.?

15 What is the next number?   4, 10, 16, ?

16 I started painting at a quarter to 11, and painted for half an hour. When did I stop?

17 Eggs are sold in boxes of ten. How many eggs are there in 7 boxes?

18 The bus had fifteen passengers. 7 got on. How many were then on the bus?

19 Danny had 28p, but he gave Chris 5p and Leroy 10p. How much did Danny have left?

20 Share 24 marbles among Tim, Tom, Ruth and Rachel. How many do they get each?

Task 24

1 What is the total of $9 + 11$?

2 From 19 take 6.

3 6×5.

4 I spend 7p out of 12p. How much have I left?

5 Share 30p among five children. How much do they each get?

6 Take ten from the smallest number here: 71, 97, 38, 49.

7 Share 120 by 10.

8 $10 = 5 + 4 + \square$.

9 Write **55** in words.

10 25×10.

11 Is this a quarter to six?

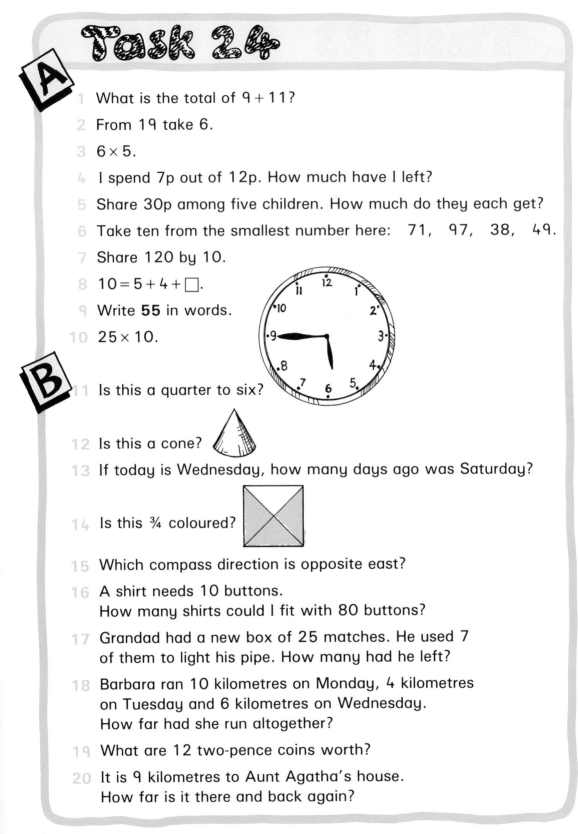

12 Is this a cone?

13 If today is Wednesday, how many days ago was Saturday?

14 Is this ¾ coloured?

15 Which compass direction is opposite east?

16 A shirt needs 10 buttons.
How many shirts could I fit with 80 buttons?

17 Grandad had a new box of 25 matches. He used 7
of them to light his pipe. How many had he left?

18 Barbara ran 10 kilometres on Monday, 4 kilometres
on Tuesday and 6 kilometres on Wednesday.
How far had she run altogether?

19 What are 12 two-pence coins worth?

20 It is 9 kilometres to Aunt Agatha's house.
How far is it there and back again?

30

The Monster

m	o	n	s	t	e	r
1	2	3	4	5	6	7

Can you use the letters of the word 'monster' to make up sums? For example,

not $= n + o + t = 3 + 2 + 5 = 10$

so **not** scores 10

1. Which word scores the most:
   one, son, or **not**?

2. Which word scores more, **rot** or **met**?

3. Which word scores more, **toe** or **ten**?

   What is the score for each of these words?

4. **nose**   5 **torn**   6 **some**   7 **rest**

8. Add up the score for the letters in **snore.**

9. Add up the score for the letters in **storm.**

10. Which word gives the better score,
    metre or **motor**?

Task 25

A

1 Add 7 to 12.

2 Take 11 from 18.

3 What are 8 lots of 3?

4 Share 24 by 4.

5 What change do I get from 20p after spending 13p?

6 Which two of these numbers add up to ten?
   1, 4, 7, 6, 8.

7 Share 240 by 10.

8 Put these in order, largest first: 42,   57,   83,   72.

9 What is the value of the two in 82?

10 Find 10 lots of 23.

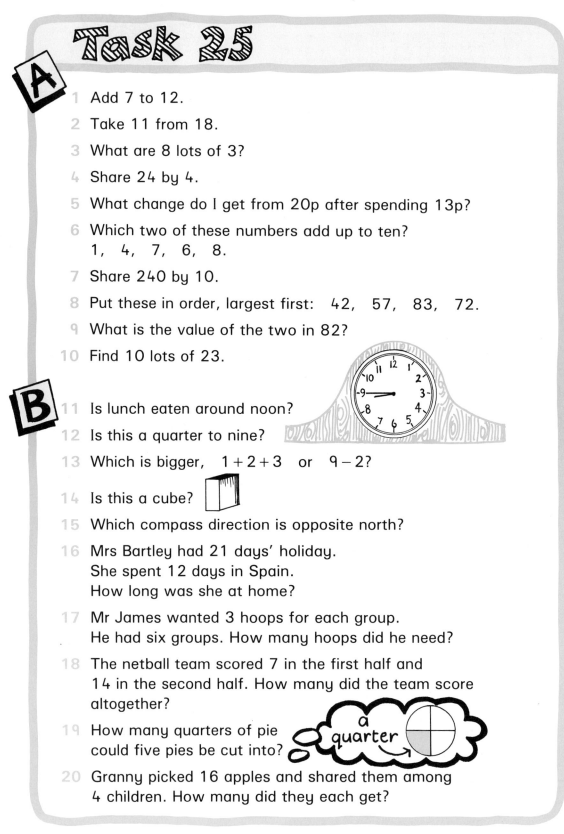

B

11 Is lunch eaten around noon?

12 Is this a quarter to nine?

13 Which is bigger, $1 + 2 + 3$ or $9 - 2$?

14 Is this a cube?

15 Which compass direction is opposite north?

16 Mrs Bartley had 21 days' holiday.
    She spent 12 days in Spain.
    How long was she at home?

17 Mr James wanted 3 hoops for each group.
    He had six groups. How many hoops did he need?

18 The netball team scored 7 in the first half and
    14 in the second half. How many did the team score
    altogether?

19 How many quarters of pie
    could five pies be cut into?

a quarter

20 Granny picked 16 apples and shared them among
    4 children. How many did they each get?

Task 26

A

1   Add together 13 and 6.

2   $14 - 9$.

3   Multiply 6 by 4.

4   Share 30 by 5.

5   Add 15p, 8p and 3p.

6   How many tens are there in 190?

7   Write **56** in words.

8   Add ten to the largest number
    here: 74, 32, 14, 81.

9   $2 + \square + 4 = 10$.

10 Take one from the smallest number
    here: 42, 38, 37, 43.

B

11 What is the next number? 10, 15, 20, ?

12 Which month has fewest days in it?

13 Is 66 an odd number?

14 Is this shape cut into quarters?

15 How long is it from 9 a.m. until 2 p.m.?

16 A farmer collects 20 eggs a day for five days.
    How many eggs does she collect altogether?

17 Dad is hanging out socks on the line. He hangs out
    8 grey ones, 2 green ones and six brown ones.
    How many is that altogether?

18 How many pies would be needed to get 12 quarters?

19 Sue was running a 26-mile marathon. When she
    reached the seven-mile stage, how much further had
    she to go?

20 Michael, Marcus and Mary each made 6 jam tarts.
    How many tarts were made altogether?

Task 27

A

1 What is the total of 17 and 6?

2 What is five less than seventeen?

3 Judy had 30p. She spent 7p. How much had she left?

4 What is 25 shared by 5?

5 A felt-tipped pen is 12 centimetres long.
How long would two felt-tipped pens measure?

6 How many tens are there in 90?

7 Multiply 17 by 10.

8 Add ten to the highest number here: 41, 34, 22, 27.

9 Write **83** in words.

10 What is 10 less than 100?

11 How many odd numbers are there between 4 and 14?

12 Which direction is opposite to east?

13 How many minutes are there between half past two
and three o'clock?

14 How many days is it from Wednesday until Monday?

15 What is the next number?   5,   8,   11,   14,   ?

16 Add together 9 and 16. Now double your answer.

17 There are 25 nails in a packet.
How many nails are in 4 packets?

18 Peter tried 20 sums. He got 7 wrong.
How many did he get right?

19 A farmer has 7 pigs, 4 goats and 15 sheep.
How many animals does he have altogether?

20 Andy had 18 conkers. Hina smashed 12 of them.
How many did Andy have left?

Task 28

A

1 Add together 7 and 22.

2 Take 5 from 14. How many are left?

3 Share 28 by 4.

4 Add 9, 9 and 4.

5 There are 6 cakes in a box.
How many cakes are there in 5 boxes?

6 What is the value of the three in 93?

7 18×10.

8 Write **91** in words.

9 Share 110 by 11.

10 Put these in order, largest
first: 42, 61, 73, 47, 59.

B

11 Write all the odd numbers between 14 and 20.

12 Is this a cylinder or a cone?

13 Which is bigger, 4×7 or $11 + 14$?

14 How long is it from 11 a.m. until 3 p.m.?

15 What is the next number? 35, 30, 25, ?

16 Marie got 16 out of 25 for a test.
How many more marks did she need to get full marks?

17 Alan had 15 toffees. Amanda ate 7 of them.
How many were left?

18 Winston had 5 red cards and 3 black ones.
James had 7 red cards and 3 black ones.
How many cards did they have altogether?

19 What is half of $7 + 9$?

20 5 pencils fill a box.
How many pencils are there in five full boxes?

Some sums with the same sun

Each triangle here has three lines of numbers.
Make each line of each triangle add up to the same
number.

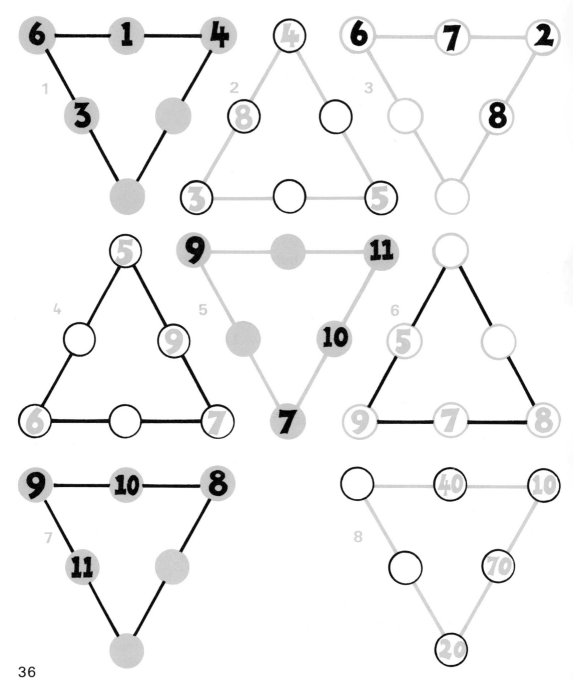

36

Task 29

1 What is 8 + 13?

2 Take 5 from 20. What is left?

3 There are 8 blue football socks on a line.
How many pairs is that?

4 30 apples are shared among six children.
How many will they each get?

5 Add together 5p, 5p, 2p and 2p.

6 What are 28 lots of 10?

7 How many 20p coins are there in £1?

8 What is ten more than the largest number
here? 42, 36, 59, 17, 39.

9 Share 190 by 10.

10 Write **seventy-six** in figures.

11 Is ¾ of this shape coloured?

12 Which four coins make 18p?

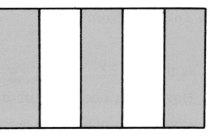

13 How many minutes are there from
half past seven until 8 o'clock?

14 Which is bigger, 8 × 3 or 5 × 5?

15 What is the next number? 21, 24, 27, 30, ?

16 A farmer had 28 eggs. If he sold half,
how many eggs would he have left?

17 What is the cost of 4 ice-lollies at 15p each?

18 A tube of sweets weighs 40 grams.
How much would two tubes weigh?

19 3 apples are cut into quarters.
How many quarters are there?

20 Dad has 20 screws to fit five shelves.
How many screws does each shelf get?

Task 30

1 Add together 19 + 5.

2 18 − 9.

3 Buttons cost 9p each. How much do 3 cost?

4 In a class of 25, eighteen can swim.
How many cannot swim?

5 I have 27 chocolate buttons to share among
three children. How many will they each get?

6 Take 10 from the largest number here: 41, 38, 72, 97

7 Write **45** in words.

8 5 + 2 + ☐ = 10.

9 How many 5p coins are there in 50p?

10 Take one from 130.

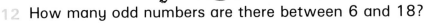

11 Is this 7:15?

12 How many odd numbers are there between 6 and 18?

13 How many halves are there in 6 whole oranges?

14 If today is Tuesday,
in how many days will it be Sunday?

15 How many minutes are there between 8:15 and 9 o'clock?

16 A car uses 28 litres of petrol in a week.
How much petrol is that for each day?

17 Add together 8 and 17. Now double your answer.

18 Ann gave three shells to each of her 3 friends, which
left her with 10 shells. How many did she start with?

19 The green team scored 6 rounders, but the red team
scored 3 times as many. How many rounders did the
red team score?

20 I have waited for 10 minutes. How much longer will
I have to wait until I have waited for half of an hour?